CHICAGO ADDRESSES

SWAMI VIVEKANANDA

Advaita Ashrama
(PUBLICATION DEPARTMENT)
5 DEHI ENTALLY ROAD · KOLKATA 700 014

Published by
Swami Tattwavidananda
Adhyaksha, Advaita Ashrama
Mayavati, Champawat, Uttarakhand, Himalayas
from its Publication Department, Kolkata
Email: mail@advaitaashrama.org
Website: www.advaitaashrama.org

Fifty-first Reprint, September 2015
10M

ISBN 978-81-7505-138-6

Printed in India at
Trio Process
Kolkata 700 014

CONTENTS

CONTENTS

Publisher's Note to the
Twenty-third Impression

In the present impression which is being
published on the occasion of the Centenary of
Swami Vivekananda's participation at the Parliament of Religions we have added a
background story of the inspiring circumstances
that made Swami Vivekananda's appearance on
the platform of the Parliament of Religions in
1893 possible. In the appendix we have
presented to our readers what many eminent
persons wrote about Swamiji and his speeches at
the Parliament. Sanskrit quotations referred to
by Swamiji in his speeches have also been

provided with in the endnotes together with their references to source-books. It is hoped that these renovations will help the readers to understand and appreciate Swami Vivekananda and his message delivered at Chicago in a deeper way.

11 September 1993   PUBLISHER

follow.

THE BACKGROUND STORY
A Wandering Monk in Search of a Way

After the passing away of Sri Ramakrishna
in August 1886, Swami Vivekananda spent
several years in intense spiritual practices, first
in the newly established Ramakrishna Mon-
astery at Baranagore, and later at other places,
such as the plains of northern India and the
Himalayas. He often wanted to enter the deepest
Indian forests to lose himself in silent meditation,
but every time some obstacle or other—sometimes the sickness of a brother monk, sometimes
the death of a devotee—brought him back to a
society beset with a thousand and one miseries.

He gradually realized that he was not meant to live the life of an ordinary recluse, struggling for personal salvation. He was destined to work for the divine mission entrusted to him by his Master, Sri Ramakrishna. The Master had told him before his passing away that he would have to do 'Mother's work', to 'teach mankind', and 'to be like a banyan tree, giving shelter to the tired, weary travelers.' At this time he felt an inner urge to wander alone over the length and breadth of India in search of a plan of action to follow.

In January 1891, leaving the company of his brother monks, he wandered from place to place, alone with God. At first he travelled in the north and later he went to the south, all the while studying closely the life of the people in every class of society. He was deeply moved by this experience. He wept to see the stagnant life of the Indian masses crushed down by ignorance and poverty, and was disturbed by the spell of materialistic ideas he noticed among the educated, who blindly imitated the glamour of the West. He saw that spirituality was at a low ebb in the land of its birth. The picture of ancient India appeared before his eyes vividly in all its grandeur and glory, and the contrast was unbearable. India should not be allowed to drift this way. He visualized that India must become dynamic in all spheres of human activity and spiritualize the life of her own children as well as all mankind. He felt that he was the instrument chosen by the Lord to bring about this change.

Some enlightened people in different parts of India had previously advised Swamiji to go to the West, where his interpretation of Hinduism might be properly appreciated. At first Swamiji did not pay much attention to them. But when he later heard about the Parliament of Religions, which was to be held in Chicago in 1893, he expressed his desire to attend it, thinking that it might help him in carrying out his divine mission.

In the last lap of his journey he came to Kannyakumari where, sitting on the prominent rock just off the main coast, he reviewed his experiences during his wanderings and meditated deeply on India—her past, present, and future, the causes of her downfall, and the means for her resurrection. All these flashed through his mind, and he took the momentous decision to go to the West to raise funds for the uplift of the Indian masses. In exchange, he decided, he would give the rich spiritual treasures that India had accumulated through the centuries and that he himself had inherited from his Master. With this decision he returned to the mainland. But still he was not sure whether the plan was in accordance with the divine will. He prayed and prayed for days together to the Mother and to his Master for guidance. Shortly afterwards, a symbolic dream convinced him that he had the needed divine command. He saw the figure of Sri Ramakrishna walking from the seashore into the ocean, beckoning him to follow. Further, Holy Mother, Sri Sarada Devi, to whom he had written earlier, sent her consent and blessings. All doubts were now gone. He was determined to go. Finally, with the money collected by his young disciples by begging from door to door as well as that given by the Maharaja of Mysore, the Raja of Ramnad, and the Raja of Khetri, Swamiji sailed for America from Mumbai (then Bombay) on 31 May 1893.

Arrival in America and Becoming a Delegate

Swamiji reached Chicago at the end of July via Colombo, Singapore, Japan and Vancouver. Arriving there he was shocked to learn from the Information Bureau that the Parliament of Religions would not commence until September and that no delegate would be admitted without proper credentials from a bona fide organization. Moreover, the time for admittance and registration of delegates was already over. Swamiji did not have any credentials whatsoever. In sending Swamiji, his disciples in Chennai (then Madras), in their unbounded enthusiasm and faith, had taken it for granted that he had only to appear and he would be given a chance. The Swami too did not foresee the difficulties in the way, as he was sure he was moving towards the fulfilment of a divine mission.

Swamiji also found that living in Chicago was very costly. As he did not have enough money, he left for Boston, where things were cheaper. On the way a wealthy traveller in the train, Miss Katherine Abbot Sanborn, was attracted by his noble bearing and charming conversation. She became more interested when she learned the purpose of his coming to America. She said: "Well, Swami, I invite you to come to my home to live. Perhaps something will turn up in your favour." The invitation was a God-send for the Swami, who readily consented and started living at her village home in Massachusetts near Boston. Through her Swamiji became acquainted with Mr. J. H. Wright, a professor of Greek at Harvard University. After a four hour conversation with Swamiji, the Professor was so impressed by his learning and wisdom that he took it upon himself to arrange for his admittance to the Parliament of Religions as a delegate. "This is the only way you can be introduced to the nation at large," he told Swamiji. Swamiji had explained his difficulties and had said that he had no credentials. Thereupon Prof. Wright had exclaimed, "To ask you, Swami, for credentials is like asking the sun to state its right to shine." He at once wrote to the Chairman of the Committee for the Selection of the Delegates, who happened to be his friend: "Here is a man who is more learned than all our professors put together." He also gave Swamiji letters of introduction to the Committee that looked after the Oriental delegates, and bought him a ticket to Chicago. Unfortunately, when Swamiji arrived in Chicago on 9 September, he found to his dismay that he had mislaid the address of the Committee. He made enquiries of passers-by, but it being the north-east side of the city where mostly Germans lived, they could not understand him. The chilly nights of September were coming on. So Swamiji, who would soon shake America by his address at the Parliament, found no other alternative than to take shelter in an empty boxcar in the railroad freight yard. He soon freed himself from all anxieties and slept there, trusting in the guidance of the Lord. In the morning he set out to find his way. He soon came to one of the rich quarters of the city. Extremely tired and hungry, he sought help from house to house as a sannyasin in India would. Seeing his soiled clothes and worn out appearance, the servants in the houses treated him rudely, sometimes slamming the door in his face. After a while, exhausted and resigning himself to the will of the Lord, he sat down on the roadside. Just then the door of a fashionable residence opposite him opened and a lady of regal appearance came out and spoke to him in a soft voice, "Sir, are you a delegate to the Parliament of Religions?" Swamiji told her of his difficulties. She at once invited him into her house and attended to his immediate needs. Later, when Swamiji had taken food and had rested, she took him to the office of the Parliament of Religions. He was gladly accepted as a delegate and lodged with the other Oriental guests. His deliverer was Mrs. George W. Hale. She and her children became Swamiji's warmest friends.

A new spirit now took possession of Swamiji. He was convinced beyond doubt that the Lord was with him. His days were spent in prayer and meditation, and in the earnest longing that he might be made a true instrument of the Lord, a true spokesman of Hinduism, a true bearer of his Master's message.

On the Platform
of the Parliament of Religions

The Parliament of Religions was an adjunct of the World's Columbian Exposition, which was held in Chicago in 1893 to celebrate the four hundredth anniversary of the discovery of America by Christopher Columbus. Some of the declared objectives of the Parliament were to present the important truths held and taught in common by different religions of the world and to bring the nations of the earth into a more friendly relationship. But many thought and hoped that the Parliament would prove the superiority of their own religion over the others. However, through divine dispensation, as it were, the validity of all religions ultimately became the keynote of the Parliament, and Swami Vivekananda became the most impressive and eloquent mouthpiece of that central theme.

The first session of the Parliament was held on Monday, 11 September 1893, in the spacious hall of the Art Institute. Its huge galleries were packed with more than 4,000 people—men and women representing the best culture of the United States. Representatives of all organized religions— Buddhism, Christianity, Confucianism, Hinduism, Jainism, Judaism, Mohammedanism, Shintoism, Theism, (Brahmo Samaj) and Zoroastrianism— were there, and among them was Swami Vivek- ananda, rapt in silent prayer, attracting the attention of the audience by his commanding presence. The Parliament opened with a prayer, after which the Chairman, Reverend J. H. Barrows, introduced the delegates one by one, who then read their prepared speeches. But Swamiji had no such written speech with him and he had never before addressed such a huge assembly. He did not speak in the morning session but went on postponing the summons from the chair. In the afternoon, when he could no longer put off his turn, he stepped up to rostrum, his face glowing like fire. Inwardly bowing down to Devi Saraswati, the Goddess of Knowledge, he began to speak. No sooner had he addressed the assembly as 'Sisters and Brothers of America' than a great wave of enthusiasm went through the audience. They rose to their feet with shouts of applause, as if they had gone mad. Everyone was cheering, cheering, and cheering. The Swami was bewildered. For two full minutes he attempted to speak, but the wild enthusiasm of the audience would not allow it. Others had addressed them in the customary manner but Swamiji had touched the deepest chord of their heart by discarding formality and stressing the kinship of all people. After the applause subsided the Swami made a brief speech.

When Swamiji had finished and sat down, exhausted with emotion, there was another tremendous ovation. The next day all the papers lionized him as the greatest figure and the best speaker of the Parliament. The unknown young monk became known throughout the United States of America. 'His life-size portraits were posted on the roadside in Chicago with his name written beneath it, and many showed reverence to it with bowed heads.'

In his speeches at the Parliament Swamiji stressed again and again the idea of validity of all religions and their harmony. Every religion, he pointed out, has produced men and women of most exalted character endowed with holiness, purity and charity. This vindicated the validity of each of them. He, therefore, appealed to every person to preserve his or her individuality and at the same time to learn and assimilate the good points, the spirit of others' religions.

Another idea that Swamiji forcefully championed at the Parliament was that man is only apparently a mortal body or a mind but is really a divine soul, a spirit, pure and immortal, the master of matter and mind. Swamiji pointed out that the goal of human life is to become divine by manifesting this divinity through our every thought and action. Herein lies the solution to all our problems—individual or collective.

We shall now present the soul-stirring lectures of Swamiji in his own words.

CHICAGO ADDRESSES

RESPONSE TO WELCOME

At the World's Parliament of Religions,
Chicago, 11 September 1893

Sisters and Brothers of America,

It fills my heart with joy unspeakable to rise in response to the warm and cordial welcome which you have given us. I thank you in the name of the most ancient order of monks in the world; I thank you in the name of the mother of religions; and I thank you in the name of the millions and millions of Hindu people of all classes and sects.

My thanks, also, to some of the speakers on this platform who, referring to the delegates from the Orient, have told you that these men from far-off nations may well claim the honour of bearing to different lands the idea of toleration. I am proud to belong to a religion which has taught the world both tolerance and universal acceptance. We believe not only in universal toleration, but we accept all religions as true. I am proud to belong to a nation which has sheltered the persecuted and the refugees of all religions and all nations of the earth. I am proud to tell you that we have gathered in our bosom the purest remnant of the Israelites, who came to southern India and took refuge with us in the very year in which their holy temple was shattered to pieces by Roman tyranny. I am proud to belong to the religion which has sheltered and is still fostering the remnant of the grand Zoroastrian nation. I will quote to you, brethren, a few lines from a hymn which I remember to have repeated from my earliest boyhood, which is every day repeated by millions of human beings: 'As the different streams having their sources in different places all mingle their water in the sea, so, O Lord, the different paths which men take through different tendencies, various though they appear, crooked or straight, all lead to Thee.'[1]

The present convention, which is one of the most august assemblies ever held, is in itself a vindication, a declaration to the world, of the wonderful doctrine preached in the Gita: 'Whosoever comes to Me, through whatsoever form, I reach him; all men are struggling through paths which in the end lead to Me.'[2] Sectarianism, bigotry, and its horrible descendant, fanaticism, have long possessed this beautiful earth. They have filled the earth with violence, drenched it often and often with human blood, destroyed civilization, and sent whole nations to despair. Had it not been for these horrible demons, human society would be far more advanced than it is now. But their time is come; and I fervently hope that the bell that tolled this morning in honour of this convention may be the death-knell of all fanaticism, of all persecutions with the sword or with the pen, and of all uncharitable feelings between persons wending their way to the same goal.

WHY WE DISAGREE

15 September 1893

I will tell you a little story. You have heard the eloquent speaker who has just finished say, 'Let us cease from abusing each other,' and he was very sorry that there should be always so much variance.

But I think I should tell you a story which would illustrate the cause of this variance. A frog lived in a well. It had lived there for a long time. It was born there and brought up there, and yet was a little, small frog. Of course the evolutionists were not there then to tell us whether the frog lost its eyes or not, but, for our story's sake, we must take it for granted that it had its eyes, and that it every day cleansed the water of all the worms and bacilli that lived in it with an energy that would do credit to our modern bacteriologists. In this way it went on and became a little sleek and fat. Well, one day another frog that lived in the sea came and fell into the well.

'Where are you from?'

'I am from the sea.'

'The sea! How big is that? Is it as big as my well?' and he took a leap from one side of the well to the other.

'My friend,' said the frog of the sea, 'how do you compare the sea with your little well?'

Then the frog took another leap and asked, 'Is your sea so big?'

'What nonsense you speak, to compare the sea with your well!'

'Well, then,' said the frog of the well, 'nothing can be bigger than my well; there can be nothing bigger than this; this fellow is a liar, so turn him out.'

That has been the difficulty all the while.

I am a Hindu. I am sitting in my own little well and thinking that the whole world is my little well. The Christian sits in his little well and thinks the whole world is his well. The Mohammedan sits in his little well and thinks that is the whole world. I have to thank you of America for the great attempt you are making to break down the barriers of this little world of ours, and hope that, in the future, the Lord will help you to accomplish your purpose.

PAPER ON HINDUISM

Read at the Parliament on 19 September 1893

Three religions now stand in the world which have come down to us from time prehistoric—Hinduism, Zoroastrianism, and Judaism. They have all received tremendous shocks, and all of them prove by their survival their internal strength. But while Judaism failed to absorb Christianity and was driven out of its place of birth by its all-conquering daughter, and a handful of Parsees is all that remains to tell the tale of their grand religion, sect after sect arose in India and seemed to shake the religion of the Vedas to its very foundations, but like the waters of the sea-shore in a tremendous earthquake it receded only for a while, only to return in an all-absorbing flood, a thousand times more vigorous, and when the tumult of the rush was over, these sects were all sucked in, absorbed, and assimilated into the immense body of the mother faith.

From the high spiritual flights of the Vedanta philosophy, of which the latest discoveries of science seem like echoes, to the low ideas of idolatry with its multifarious mythology, the agnosticism of the Buddhists, and the atheism of the Jains, each and all have a place in the Hindu's religion.

Where then, the question arises, where is the common centre to which all these widely diverging radii converge? Where is the common basis upon which all these seemingly hopeless contradictions rest? And this is the question I shall attempt to answer.

The Hindus have received their religion through revelation, the Vedas. They hold that the Vedas are without beginning and without end. It may sound ludicrous to this audience, how a book can be without beginning or end. But by the Vedas no books are meant. They mean the accumulated treasury of spiritual laws discovered by different persons in different times. Just as the law of gravitation existed before its discovery, and would exist if all humanity forgot it, so is it with the laws that govern the spiritual world. The moral, ethical, and spiritual relations between soul and soul and between individual spirits and the Father of all spirits, were there before their discovery, and would remain even if we forgot them.

The discoverers of these laws are called Rishis, and we honour them as perfected beings. I am glad to tell this audience that some of the very greatest of them were women. Here it may be said that these laws as laws may be without end, but they must have had a beginning. The Vedas teach us that creation is without beginning or end. Science is said to have proved that the sum total of cosmic energy is always the same. Then, if there was a time when nothing existed, where was all this manifested energy? Some say it was in a potential form in God. In that case God is sometimes potential and sometimes kinetic, which would make Him mutable. Everything mutable is a compound, and everything compound must undergo that change which is called destruction. So God would die, which is absurd. Therefore there never was a time when there was no creation.

If I may be allowed to use a simile, creation and creator are two lines, without beginning and without end, running parallel to each other. God is the ever active providence, by whose power systems after systems are being evolved out of chaos, made to run for a time, and again destroyed. This is what the Brahmin boy repeats every day: 'The sun and the moon, the Lord created like the suns and moons of previous cycles.'[3] And this agrees with modern science.

Here I stand and if I shut my eyes, and try to conceive my existence, 'I,' 'I,' 'I,' what is the idea before me? The idea of a body. Am I, then, nothing but a combination of material substances? The Vedas declare, 'No.' I am a spirit living in a body. I am not the body. The body will die, but I shall not die. Here I am in this body; it will fall, but I shall go on living. I had also a past. The soul was not created, for creation means a combination which means a certain future dissolution. If then the soul was created, it must die. Some are born happy, enjoy perfect health, with beautiful body, mental vigour, and all wants supplied. Others are born miserable, some are without hands or feet, others again are idiots and only drag on a wretched existence. Why, if they are all created, why does a just and merciful God create one happy and another unhappy, why is He so partial? Nor would it mend matters in the least to hold that those who are miserable in this life will be happy in a future one. Why should a man be miserable even here in the reign of a just and merciful God?

In the second place, the idea of a creator God does not explain the anomaly, but simply expresses the cruel fiat of an all-powerful being. There must have been causes, then, before his birth, to make a man miserable or happy and those were his past actions.

Are not all the tendencies of the mind and the body accounted for by inherited aptitude?

Here are two parallel lines of existence—one of the mind, the other of matter. If matter and its transformations answer for all that we have, there is no necessity for supposing the existence of a soul. But it cannot be proved that thought has been evolved out of matter, and if a philosophical monism is inevitable, spiritual monism is certainly logical and no less desirable than a materialistic monism; but neither of these is necessary here.

We cannot deny that bodies acquire certain tendencies from heredity, but those tendencies only mean the physical configuration, through which a peculiar mind alone can act in a peculiar way. There are other tendencies peculiar to a soul caused by his past actions. And a soul with a certain tendency would by the laws of affinity take birth in a body which is the fittest instrument for the display of that tendency. This is in accord with science, for science wants to explain everything by habit, and habit is got through repetitions. So repetitions are necessary to explain the natural habits of a new-born soul. And since they were not obtained in this present life, they must have come down from past lives.

There is another suggestion. Taking all these for granted, how is it that I do not remember anything of my past life? This can be easily explained. I am now speaking English. It is not my mother tongue, in fact no words of my mother tongue are now present in my consciousness; but let me try to bring them up, and they rush in. That shows that consciousness is only the surface of the mental ocean, and within its depths are stored up all our experiences. Try and struggle, they would come up and you would be conscious even of your past life.

This is direct and demonstrative evidence. Verification is the perfect proof of a theory, and here is the challenge thrown to the world by the Rishis. We have discovered the secret by which the very depths of the ocean of memory can be stirred up—try it and you would get a complete reminiscence of your past life.

So then the Hindu believes that he is a spirit. Him the sword cannot pierce—him the fire cannot burn—him the water cannot melt—him the air cannot dry.[4] The Hindu believes that every soul is a circle whose circumference is nowhere, but whose centre is located in the body, and that death means the change of this centre from body to body. Nor is the soul bound by the conditions of matter. In its very essence, it is free, unbounded, holy, pure, and perfect. But somehow or other it finds itself tied down to matter, and thinks of itself as matter.

Why should the free, perfect, and pure being be thus under the thraldom of matter, is the next question. How can the perfect soul be deluded into the belief that it is imperfect? We have been told that the Hindus shirk the question and say that no such question can be there. Some thinkers want to answer it by positing one or more quasi-perfect beings, and use big scientific names to fill up the gap. But naming is not explaining. The question remains the same. How can the perfect become the quasi-perfect; how can the pure, the absolute change even a microscopic particle of its nature? But the Hindu is sincere. He does not want to take shelter under sophistry. He is brave enough to face the question in a manly fashion; and his answer is: 'I do not know. I do not know how the perfect being, the soul, came to think of itself as imperfect, as joined to and conditioned by matter.' But the fact is a fact for all that. It is a fact in everybody's consciousness that one thinks of oneself as the body. The Hindu does not attempt to explain why one thinks one is the body. The answer that it is the will of God is no explanation. This is nothing more than what the Hindu says, 'I do not know.'

Well, then, the human soul is eternal and immortal, perfect and infinite, and death means only a change of centre from one body to another. The present is determined by our past actions, and the future by the present. The soul will go on evolving up or reverting back from birth to birth and death to death. But here is another question: Is man a tiny boat in a tempest, raised one moment on the foamy crest of a billow and dashed down into a yawning chasm the next, rolling to and fro at the mercy of good and bad actions—a powerless, helpless wreck in an ever-raging, ever-rushing, uncompromising current of cause and effect, a little moth placed under the wheel of causation, which rolls on crushing everything in its way and waits not for the widow's tears or the orphan's cry ? The heart sinks at the idea, yet this is the law of nature. Is there no hope? Is there no escape?—was the cry that went up from the bottom of the heart of despair. It reached the throne of mercy, and words of hope and consolation came down and inspired a Vedic sage, and he stood up before the world and in trumpet voice proclaimed the glad tidings: 'Hear, ye children of immortal bliss! even ye that reside in higher spheres! I have found the Ancient One who is beyond all darkness, all delusion: knowing Him alone you shall be saved from death over again.' [5] 'Children of immortal bliss'—what a sweet, what a hopeful name! Allow me to call you, brethren, by that sweet name—heirs of immortal bliss—yea, the Hindu refuses to call you sinners. Ye are the Children of God, the sharers of immortal bliss, holy and perfect beings. Ye divinities on earth—sinners! It is a sin to call a man so; it is a standing libel on human nature. Come up, O lions, and shake off the delusion that you are sheep; you are souls immortal, spirits free, blest and eternal; ye are not matter, ye are not bodies; matter is your servant, not you the servant of matter.

Thus it is that the Vedas proclaim not a dreadful combination of unforgiving laws, not an endless prison of cause and effect, but that at the head of all these laws, in and through every particle of matter and force, stands One, 'by whose command the wind blows, the fire burns, the clouds rain, and death stalks upon the earth'.[6]

And what is His nature?

He is everywhere, the pure and formless One, the Almighty and the All-merciful. 'Thou art our father, Thou art our mother, Thou art our beloved friend. Thou art the source of all strength; give us strength. Thou art He that beareth the burdens of the universe; help me bear the little burden of this life.' Thus sang the Rishis of the Veda. And how to worship Him? Through love. 'He is to be worshipped as the one beloved, dearer than everything in this and the next life.'

This is the doctrine of love declared in the Vedas, and let us see how it is fully developed and taught by Krishna, whom the Hindus believe to have been God incarnate on earth.

He taught that a man ought to live in this world like a lotus leaf, which grows in water but is never moistened by water; so a man ought to live in the world—his heart to God and his hands to work.

It is good to love God for hope of reward in this or the next world, but it is better to love God for love's sake, and the prayer goes: 'Lord, I do not want wealth, nor children, nor learning. If it be Thy will, I shall go from birth to birth, but grant me this, that I may love Thee without the hope of reward—love unselfishly for love's sake.'[7] One of the disciples of Krishna, the then Emperor of India, was driven from his kingdom by his enemies and had to take shelter with his queen, in a forest in the Himalayas, and there one day the queen asked him how it was that he, the most virtuous of men, should suffer so much misery. Yudhishthira answered, 'Behold, my queen, the Himalayas, how grand and beautiful they are; I love them. They do not give me anything, but my nature is to love the grand, the beautiful, therefore I love them. Similarly, I love the Lord. He is the source of all beauty, of all sublimity. He is the only object to be loved; my nature is to love Him, and therefore I love. I do not pray for anything; I do not ask for anything. Let Him place me wherever He likes. I must love Him for love's sake. I cannot trade in love.' [8]

The Vedas teach that the soul is divine, only held in the bondage of matter; perfection will be reached when this bond will burst, and the word they use for it is therefore, Mukti—freedom, freedom from the bonds of imperfection, freedom from death and misery.

And this bondage can only fall off through the mercy of God, and this mercy comes on the pure. So purity is the condition of His mercy. How does that mercy act? He reveals Himself to the pure heart; the pure and the stainless see God, yea, even in this life; then and then only all the crookedness of the heart is made straight. Then all doubt ceases. [9] He is no more the freak of a terrible law of causation. This is the very centre, the very vital conception of Hinduism. The Hindu does not want to live upon words and theories. If there are existences beyond the ordinary sensuous existence, he wants to come face to face with them. If there is a soul in him which is not matter, if there is an all-merciful universal Soul, he will go to Him direct. He must see Him, and that alone can destroy all doubts. So the best proof a Hindu sage gives about the soul, about God, is: 'I have seen the soul; I have seen God.' And that is the only condition of perfection. The Hindu religion does not consist in struggles and attempts to believe a certain doctrine or dogma, but in realizing—not in believing, but in being and becoming.

Thus the whole object of their system is by constant struggle to become perfect, to become divine, to reach God, and see God, and this reaching God, seeing God, becoming perfect even as the Father in Heaven is perfect, constitutes the religion of the Hindus.

And what becomes of a man when he attains perfection? He lives a life of bliss infinite. He enjoys infinite and perfect bliss, having obtained the only thing in which man ought to have pleasure, namely God, and enjoys the bliss with God.

So far all the Hindus are agreed. This is the common religion of all the sects of India; but, then, perfection is absolute, and the absolute cannot be two or three. It cannot have any qualities. It cannot be an individual. And so when a soul becomes perfect and absolute, it must become one with Brahman, and it would only realize the Lord as the perfection, the reality, of its own nature and existence, the existence absolute, knowledge absolute, and bliss absolute. We have often and often read this called the losing of individuality and becoming a stock or a stone.

'He jests at scars that never felt a wound.'

I tell you it is nothing of the kind. If it is happiness to enjoy the consciousness of this small body, it must be greater happiness to enjoy the consciousness of two bodies, the measure of happiness increasing with the consciousness of an increasing number of bodies, the aim, the ultimate of happiness being reached when it would become a universal consciousness.

Therefore, to gain this infinite universal individuality, this miserable little prison-individuality must go. Then alone can death cease when I am one with life, then alone can misery cease when I am one with happiness itself, then alone can all errors cease when I am one with knowledge itself; and this is the necessary scientific conclusion. Science has proved to me that physical individuality is a delusion, that really my body is one little continuously changing body in an unbroken ocean of matter; and Advaita (unity) is the necessary conclusion with my other counterpart, Soul.

Science is nothing but the finding of unity. As soon as science would reach perfect unity, it would stop from further progress, because it would reach the goal. Thus chemistry could not progress farther when it would discover one element out of which all others could be made. Physics would stop when it would be able to fulfil its services in discovering one energy of which all the others are but manifestations, and the science of religion become perfect when it would discover Him who is the one life in a universe of death, Him who is the constant basis of an ever-changing world, One who is the only Soul of which all souls are but delusive manifestations. Thus is it, through multiplicity and duality, that the ultimate unity is reached. Religion can go no farther. This is the goal of all science.

All science is bound to come to this conclusion in the long run. Manifestation, and not creation, is the word of science today, and the Hindu is only glad that what he has been cherishing in his bosom for ages is going to be taught in more forcible language, and with further light from the latest conclusions of science.

Descend we now from the aspirations of philosophy to the religion of the ignorant. At the very outset, I may tell you that there is no *polytheism* in India. In every temple, if one stands by and listens, one will find the worshippers applying all the attributes of God, including omnipresence, to the images. It is not polytheism, nor would the name henotheism explain the situation. 'The rose, called by any other name, would smell as sweet.' Names are not explanations.

I remember, as a boy, hearing a Christian missionary preach to a crowd in India. Among other sweet things he was telling them was that if he gave a blow to their idol with his stick, what could it do? One of his hearers sharply answered, 'If I abuse your God, what can He do?' 'You would be punished,' said the preacher, 'when you die.' 'So my idol will punish you when you die,' retorted the Hindu.

The tree is known by its fruits. When I have seen amongst them that are called idolaters, men, the like of whom, in morality and spirituality and love I have never seen anywhere, I stop and ask myself, 'Can sin beget holiness?'

Superstition is a great enemy of man, but bigotry is worse. Why does a Christian go to church? Why is the cross holy? Why is the face turned toward the sky in prayer? Why are there so many images in the Catholic Church? Why are there so many images in the minds of Protestants when they pray? My brethren, we can no more think about anything without a mental image than we can live without breathing. By the law of association the material image calls up the mental idea and vice versa. This is why the Hindu uses an external symbol when he worships. He will tell you, it helps to keep his mind fixed on the Being to whom he prays. He knows as well as you do that the image is not God, is not omnipresent. After all, how much does omnipresence mean to almost the whole world? It stands merely as a word, a symbol. Has God superficial area? If not, when we repeat that word 'omnipresent', we think of the extended sky or of space, that is all.

As we find that somehow or other, by the laws of our mental constitution, we have to associate our ideas of infinity with the image of the blue sky, or of the sea, so we naturally connect our idea of holiness with the image of a church, a mosque, or a cross. The Hindus have associated the ideas of holiness, purity, truth, omnipresence, and such other ideas with different images and forms. But with this difference that while some people devote their whole lives to their idol of a church and never rise higher, because with them religion means an intellectual assent to certain doctrines and doing good to their fellows, the whole religion of the Hindu is centred in realization. Man is to become divine by realizing the divine. Idols or temples or churches or books are only the supports, the helps, of his spiritual childhood; but on and on he must progress.

He must not stop anywhere. 'External worship, material worship,' say the scriptures, 'is the lowest stage; struggling to rise high, mental prayer is the next stage, but the highest stage is when the Lord has been realized.' [10] Mark, the same earnest man who is kneeling before the idol tells you, 'Him the sun cannot express, nor the moon, nor the stars, the lightning cannot express Him, nor what we speak of as fire; through Him they shine.' [11] But he does not abuse any one's idol or call its worship sin. He recognizes in it a necessary stage of life. 'The child is father of the man.' Would it be right for an old man to say that childhood is a sin or youth a sin?

If a man can realize his divine nature with the help of an image, would it be right to call that a sin? Nor, even when he has passed that stage, should he call it an error. To the Hindu, man is not travelling from error to truth, but from truth to truth, from lower to higher truth. To him all the religions, from the lowest fetishism to the highest absolutism, mean so many attempts of the human soul to grasp and realize the Infinite, each determined by the conditions of its birth and association, and each of these marks a stage of progress; and every soul is a young eagle soaring higher and higher, gathering more and more strength, till it reaches the Glorious Sun.

Unity in variety is the plan of nature, and the Hindu has recognized it. Every other religion lays down certain fixed dogmas, and tries to force society to adopt them. It places before society only one coat which must fit Jack and John and Henry, all alike. If it does not fit John or Henry, he must go without a coat to cover his body. The Hindus have discovered that the absolute can only be realized, or thought of, or stated, through the relative, and the images, crosses, and crescents are simply so many symbols—so many pegs to hang spiritual ideas on. It is not that this help is necessary for everyone, but those that do not need it have no right to say that it is wrong. Nor is it compulsory in Hinduism.

One thing I must tell you. Idolatry in India does not mean anything horrible. It is not the mother of harlots. On the other hand, it is the attempt of undeveloped minds to grasp high spiritual truths. The Hindus have their faults, they sometimes have their exceptions; but mark this, they are always for punishing their own bodies, and never for cutting the throats of their neighbours. If the Hindu fanatic burns himself on the pyre, he never lights the fire of Inquisition. And even this cannot be laid at the door of his religion any more than the burning of witches can be laid at the door of Christianity.

To the Hindu, then, the whole world of religions is only a travelling, a coming up, of different men and women, through various conditions and circumstances, to the same goal. Every religion is only evolving a God out of the material man, and the same God is the inspirer of all of them. Why, then, are there so many contradictions? They are only apparent, says the Hindu. The contradictions come from the same truth adapting itself to the varying circumstances of different natures.

It is the same light coming through glasses

of different colours. And these little variations are necessary for purposes of adaptation. But in the heart of everything the same truth reigns. The Lord has declared to the Hindu in His incarnation as Krishna: 'I am in every religion as the thread through a string of pearls.[12] Wherever thou seest extraordinary holiness and extraordinary power raising and purifying humanity, know thou that I am there.'[13] And what has been the result? I challenge the world to find, throughout the whole system of Sanskrit philosophy, any such expression as that the Hindu alone will be saved and not others. Says Vyasa, 'We find perfect men even beyond the pale of our caste and creed.'[14] One thing more. How, then, can the Hindu, whose whole fabric of thought centres in God, believe in Buddhism which is agnostic, or in Jainism which is atheistic?

The Buddhists or the Jains do not depend upon God; but the whole force of their religion is directed to the great central truth in every religion, to evolve a God out of man. They have not seen the Father, but they have seen the Son. And he that hath seen the Son hath seen the Father also.

This, brethren, is a short sketch of the religious ideas of the Hindus. The Hindu may have failed to carry out all his plans, but if there is ever to be a universal religion, it must be one which will have no location in place or time; which will be infinite like the God it will preach, and whose sun will shine upon the followers of Krishna and of Christ, on saints and sinners alike; which will not be Brahminic or Buddhistic, Christian or Mohammedan, but the sum total of all these, and still have infinite space for development; which in its catholicity will embrace in its infinite arms, and find a place for, every human being, from the lowest grovelling savage not far removed from the brute, to the highest man towering by the virtues of his head and heart almost above humanity, making society stand in awe of him and doubt his human nature. It will be a religion which will have no place for persecution or intolerance in its polity, which will recognize divinity in every man and woman, and whose whole scope, whose whole force, will be centred in aiding humanity to realize its own true, divine nature.

Offer such a religion, and all the nations will follow you. Asoka's council was a council of the Buddhist faith. Akbar's, though more to the purpose, was only a parlour meeting. It was reserved for America to proclaim to all quarters of the globe that the Lord is in every religion.

May He who is the Brahman of the Hindus, the Ahura-Mazda of the Zoroastrians, the Buddha of the Buddhists, the Jehovah of the Jews, the Father in Heaven of the Christians, give strength to you to carry out your noble idea! The star arose in the East; it travelled steadily towards the West, sometimes dimmed and sometimes effulgent, till it made a circuit of the world; and now it is again rising on the very horizon of the East, the borders of the Sanpo*, a thousandfold more effulgent than it ever was before.

---

* A Tibetan name for the Brahmaputra River. According to *The World's Parliament of Religions* (Chicago: The Parliament Publishing Company, 1893), vol. II, p. 978, the word is 'Tasifu'. Marie Louise Burke in her book *Swami Vivekananda in the West: New Discoveries: His Prophetic Mission* (Mayavati: Advaita Ashrama, 1983), vol. I, pp. 143-44, opines that the word should be 'Pacific'.

Hail Columbia, motherland of liberty! It has been given to thee, who never dipped her hand in her neighbour's blood, who never found out that the shortest way of becoming rich was by robbing one's neighbours, it has been given to thee to march at the vanguard of civilization with the flag of harmony.

RELIGION NOT THE CRYING NEED OF INDIA

20 September 1893

Christians must always be ready for good criticism, and I hardly think that you will mind if I make a little criticism. You Christians, who are so fond of sending out missionaries to save the soul of the heathen—why do you not try to save their bodies from starvation? In India, during the terrible famines, thousands died from hunger, yet you Christians did nothing. You erect churches all through India, but the crying evil in

the East is not religion—they have religion
enough—but it is bread that the suffering millions of burning India cry out for with parched
throats. They ask us for bread, but we give them
stones. It is an insult to a starving people to offer
them religion; it is an insult to a starving man to
teach him metaphysics. In India a priest that
preached for money would lose caste and be
spat upon by the people. I came here to seek aid
for my impoverished people, and I fully realized
how difficult it was to get help for heathens from
Christians in a Christian land.

BUDDHISM : THE
FULFILMENT OF HINDUISM

26 September 1893

I am not a Buddhist, as you have heard, and
yet I am. If China, or Japan, or Ceylon follow the
teachings of the Great Master, India worships
him as God incarnate on earth. You have just now
heard that I am going to criticize Buddhism, but
by that I wish you to understand only this. Far be
it from me to criticize him whom I worship as
God incarnate on earth. But our views about
Buddha are that he was not understood properly
by his disciples. The relation between Hinduism

(by Hinduism, I mean the religion of the Vedas) and what is called Buddhism at the present day is nearly the same as between Judaism and Christianity. Jesus Christ was a Jew, and Shakya Muni was a Hindu. The Jews rejected Jesus Christ, nay, crucified him, and the Hindus have accepted Shakya Muni as God and worship him. But the real difference that we Hindus want to show between modern Buddhism and what we should understand as the teachings of Lord Buddha lies principally in this: Shakya Muni came to preach nothing new. He also, like Jesus, came to fulfil and not to destroy. Only, in the case of Jesus, it was the old people, the Jews, who did not understand him, while in the case of Buddha, it was his own followers who did not realize the import of his teachings. As the Jew did not understand the fulfilment of the Old Testament, so the Buddhist did not understand the fulfilment of the truths of the Hindu religion. Again, I repeat, Shakya Muni came not to destroy, but he was the fulfilment, the logical conclusion, the logical development of the religion of the Hindus.

The religion of the Hindus is divided into two parts: the ceremonial and the spiritual. The spiritual portion is specially studied by the monks.

In that there is no caste. A man from the highest caste and a man from the lowest may become a monk in India, and the two castes become equal. In religion there is no caste; caste is simply a social institution. Shakya Muni himself was a monk, and it was his glory that he had the large-heartedness to bring out the truths from the hidden Vedas and throw them broadcast all over the world. He was the first being in the world who brought missionarizing into practice—nay, he was the first to conceive the idea of proselytizing.

The great glory of the Master lay in his wonderful sympathy for everybody, especially for the ignorant and the poor. Some of his disciples were Brahmins. When Buddha was teaching, Sanskrit was no more the spoken language in India. It was then only in the books of the learned. Some of Buddha's Brahmin disciples wanted to translate his teachings into Sanskrit, but he distinctly told them, 'I am for the poor, for the people: let me speak in the tongue

of the people.' And so to this day the great bulk
of his teachings are in the vernacular of that day
in India.

Whatever may be the position of
philosophy, whatever may be the position of
metaphysics, so long as there is such a thing as
death in the world, so long as there is such a
thing as weakness in the human heart, so long as
there is a cry going out of the heart of man in his
very weakness, there shall be a faith in God.

On the philosophic side the disciples of the
Great Master dashed themselves against the
eternal rocks of the Vedas and could not crush
them, and on the other side they took away from
the nation that eternal God to which everyone,
man or woman, clings so fondly. And the result
was that Buddhism had to die a natural death in
India. At the present day there is not one who
calls oneself a Buddhist in India, the land of its
birth.

But at the same time, Brahminism lost
something—that reforming zeal, that wonderful
sympathy and charity for everybody, that
wonderful leaven which Buddhism had brought

to the masses and which had rendered Indian society so great that a Greek historian who wrote about India of that time was led to say that no Hindu was known to tell an untruth and no Hindu woman was known to be unchaste.

Hinduism cannot live without Buddhism, nor Buddhism without Hinduism. Then realize what the separation has shown to us, that the Buddhists cannot stand without the brain and philosophy of the Brahmins, nor the Brahmin without the heart of the Buddhist. This separation between the Buddhists and the Brahmins is the cause of the downfall of India. That is why India is populated by three hundred millions of beggars, and that is why India has been the slave of conquerors for the last thousand years. Let us then join the wonderful intellect of the Brahmin with the heart, the noble soul, the wonderful humanizing power of the Great Master.

ADDRESS AT THE FINAL SESSION

27 September 1893

The World's Parliament of Religions has become an accomplished fact, and the merciful Father has helped those who laboured to bring it into existence, and crowned with success their most unselfish labour.

My thanks to those noble souls whose large hearts and love of truth first dreamed this wonderful dream and then realized it. My thanks to the shower of liberal sentiments that has overflowed this platform. My thanks to this enlightened audience for their uniform kindness to me and for their appreciation of every thought that tends to smooth the friction of religions. A few jarring notes were heard from time to time in this harmony. My special thanks to them, for they have, by their striking contrast, made the general harmony the sweeter.

Much has been said of the common ground of religious unity. I am not going just now to venture my own theory. But if anyone here hopes that this unity will come by the triumph of any one of the religions and the destruction of the others, to him I say, 'Brother, yours is an impossible hope.' Do I wish that the Christian would become Hindu? God forbid. Do I wish that the Hindu or Buddhist would become Christian? God forbid.

The seed is put in the ground, and earth and air and water are placed around it. Does the seed become the earth, or the air, or the water? No. It becomes a plant, it develops after the law of its own growth, assimilates the air, the earth, and the water, converts them into plant substance, and grows into a plant.

Similar is the case with religion. The Christian is not to become a Hindu or a Buddhist, nor a Hindu or a Buddhist to become a Christian. But each must assimilate the spirit of the others and yet preserve his individuality and grow according to his own law of growth.

If the Parliament of Religions has shown anything to the world it is this: It has proved to the world that holiness, purity and charity are not the exclusive possessions of any church in the world, and that every system has produced men and women of the most exalted character. In the face of this evidence, if anybody dreams of the exclusive survival of his own religion and the destruction of the others, I pity him from the bottom of my heart, and point out to him that upon the banner of every religion will soon be written, in spite of resistance: 'Help and not Fight', 'Assimilation and not Destruction', 'Harmony and Peace and not Dissension'.

APPENDIX

What they said of Swamiji and his speeches

Swami Vivekananda exercised a wonderful influence over his audience.

—Dr. J. H. Barrows
Chairman of General Committee of the
Parliament of Religions, Chicago.

. . . by far the most important and typical representative of Hinduism was Swami

Vivekananda, who in fact was beyond question the most popular and influential man in the Parliament.

—Mr. Merwin-Marie Snell
President of Scientific Section of the
Parliament of Religions, Chicago.

He is undoubtedly the greatest figure in the Parliament of Religions. After hearing him we feel how foolish it is to send missionaries to this learned nation.

—*The New York Herald.*

Vivekananda's address before the Parliament was broad as the heaven above us, embracing the best in all religions, as the ultimate universal religion—charity to all mankind and good works for the love of God, not for fear of punishment or hope of reward. He is a great favourite of the Parliament. . . . If he merely crosses the platform he is applauded. . . . At the Parliament of Religions they used to keep

Vivekananda until the end of the programme to make people stay till the end of the session. . . .The four thousand fanning people in the Hall of Columbus would sit smiling and expectant waiting for an hour or two to listen to Vivekananda for fifteen minutes. The Chairman knew the old rule of keeping the best until the last.

—*Boston Evening Transcript.*

Of the Swami's address before the Parliament of Religions, it may be said that when he began to speak it was of 'the religious ideas of the Hindus', but when he ended, Hinduism had been created.

For it was no experience of his own that rose to the lips of the Swami Vivekananda there. He did not even take advantage of the occasion to tell the story of his Master. Instead of either of these, it was the religious consciousness of India that spoke through him, the message of his whole people, as determined by their whole past. . . .

Others stood beside the Swami Vivekananda, on the same platform as he, as apostles of particular creeds and churches. But it was his glory that he came to preach a religion to which each of these was, in his own words, "only a travelling, a coming up, of different men and women, through various conditions and circumstances to the same goal".

—Sister Nivedita (Miss Margaret E. Noble)
in her Introduction to
The Complete Works of Swami Vivekananda.

Swami Vivekananda's participation and his magisterial and at the same time sweet and reasonable pronouncements at the International Congress of Religions at Chicago in 1893 form a very important event in the intellectual history of modern man. There he proclaimed for the first time the necessity for a new and enlightened kind of religious understanding and toleration. Although the ordinary run of people are not conscious of it, the message which was given out by Vivekananda to America and the Western World at Chicago in 1893, and subsequently to people in America, England and India, has been an effective force in the liberalization of the human spirit in its religious approach.

—Suniti Kumar Chatterjee
Swami Vivekananda Centenary Memorial Volume,
pp. 228-33.

On Monday, September 11, 1893, the first session of the Parliament was opened. . . . but it was the young man [Vivekananda] who represented nothing—and everything—the man belonging to no sect, but rather to India as a whole, who drew the glance of the assembled thousands. . . . his speech was like a tongue of flame, it fired the souls of the listening throng. . . .

Each of the other orators had spoken of his God, of the God of his sect. He— he alone— spoke of all their Gods, and embraced them all in the Universal Being. It was the breath of Ramakrishna, breaking down the barriers through the mouth of his great disciple. . . . During the ensuing days he spoke again ten or twelve times. Each time he repeated with new arguments but

5

with the same force of conviction his thesis of a universal religion without limit of time or space, uniting the whole Credo of human spirit from the enslaved fetishism of the savage to the most liberal creative affirmations of modern science. He harmonised them into a magnificent synthesis which. . . . helped all hopes to grow and flourish according to their own proper nature. There was to be no other dogma but the divinity inherent in man and his capacity of indefinite evolution. . . .

The effect of these mighty words was immense. Over the heads of the official representatives of the Parliament they were addressed to all and appealed to outside thought. Vivekananda's fame at once spread abroad, and India as a whole benefited. . . .

—Romain Rolland
The Life of Swami Vivekananda, pp. 36-40.

The visit of Swami Vivekananda to America and the subsequent work of those who followed him did more for India than a hundred

London Congresses could effect. That is the true way of awakening sympathy—by showing ourselves to the nations as a people with a great past and an ancient civilization who still possess something of the genius and character of our forefathers, have still something to give to the world and therefore deserve freedom—by manliness and fitness, not by mendicancy.

The going forth of Swami Vivekananda marked out by the Master as the heroic soul destined to take the world between his two hands and change it, was the first visible sign to the world that India was awake not only to survive but to conquer. Once the soul of the nation was awake in religion, it was only a matter of time and opportunity for it to throw on all spiritual and intellectual activities in national existence and take possession of them.

—Sri Aurobindo
in *Sri Aurobindo* (Sri Aurobindo
Birth Centenary Library, Pondicherry)
Vol. 2 (1972) pp. 37 and 171.

The spirit that reigned over the Parliament and dominated the soul of almost every religious representative present, was that of universal toleration and universal deliverance, and it ought to be a matter of pride to India, to all Hindus specially, that no one expressed, as the American papers say, this spirit so well as the Hindu representative, Swami Vivekananda. His address, in every way worthy of the representative of a religion, such as Hinduism is, struck the keynote of the Parliament of Religion. . . . The spirit of catholicity and toleration which distinguishes Hinduism, forming one of its broad features, was never before so prominently brought to the notice of the world, as it has been by Swami Vivekananda, and we make no doubt that the Swami's address will have an effect on other religions, whose teachers, preachers and Missionaries heard him, and were impressed by his utterances.

—*Indian Mirror* (21 March 1894)
Quoted in *The Life of Swami Vivekananda*
Vol. I (1979), page 437.

A striking figure, clad in yellow and orange, shining like the sun of India in the midst of the heavy atmosphere of Chicago, a lion head, piercing eyes, mobile lips, movements swift and abrupt—such was my first impression of Swami Vivekananda, as I met him in one of the rooms set apart for the use of the delegates to the Parliament of Religion.

Enraptured, the huge multitude hung upon his words; not a syllable must be lost, not a cadence missed! "That man a heathen!" said one, as he came out of the great hall, "and we send missionaries to his people! It would be more fitting that they should send missionaries to us."

—Dr. Annie Besant
Quoted in *The Life of Swami Vivekananda*
Vol. I (1979), page 429.

In his deep voice, he began, 'Sisters and Brothers of America' —and the entire audience, many hundred people, clapped and cheered wildly for two whole minutes. . . . No doubt the vast majority of those present hardly knew why they had been so powerfully moved. The appearance, even the voice, of Vivekananda cannot fully explain it. A large gathering has its own strange kind of subconscious telepathy, and this one must have been somehow aware that it was in the presence of that most unusual of beings, a man whose words express exactly what he is. When Vivekananda said, 'Sisters and Brothers' he actually meant that he regarded the American women and men before him as sisters and brothers; the well-known orational phrase became simple truth.

—by Christopher Isherwood
in *What Religion Is in the words of Swami
Vivekananda*, (1991) page XVI.

REFERENCES

1.   रुचीनां वैचित्र्यादृजुकुटिलनानापथजुषां ।
     नृणामेको गम्यस्त्वमसि पयसामर्णव इव ॥
                     Śiva Mahimnaḥ Stotram, 7

2. ये यथा मां प्रपद्यन्ते तांस्तथैव भजाम्यहम् ।
   मम वर्त्मानुवर्तन्ते मनुष्याः पार्थ सर्वशः ॥

   Gītā, 4.11

3. सूर्याचन्द्रमसौ धाता यथापूर्वमकल्पयत् ।

   Ṛg Veda, 10.190

4. नैनं छिन्दन्ति शस्त्राणि नैनं दहति पावकः ।
   न चैनं क्लेदयन्त्यापो न शोषयति मारुतः ॥

   Gītā, 2.23

5. शृण्वन्तु विश्वे अमृतस्य पुत्रा
   आ ये धामानि दिव्यानि तस्थुः ॥

   ...   .

   वेदाहमेतं पुरुषं महान्त-
   मादित्यवर्णं तमसः परस्तात् ।
   तमेव विदित्वाऽतिमृत्युमेति
   नान्यः पन्था विद्यतेऽयनाय ॥

   Śvetāśvatara Upaniṣad, 2.5, 3.8

6. भयादस्याग्निस्तपति भयात्तपति सूर्यः ।
   भयादिन्द्रश्च वायुश्च मृत्युर्धावति पंचमः ॥

   Kaṭhopaniṣad, 2.3.3

7. न धनं न जनं न सुन्दरीं कवितां वा जगदीश कामये ।
   मम जन्मनि जन्मनीश्वरे भवताद् भक्तिरहैतुकी त्वयि ॥

   Śikṣāṣṭakam, 4

8. नाहं कर्मफलान्वेषी राजपुत्रि चराम्युत ।
    ददामि देयमित्येव यजे यष्टव्यमित्युत ॥
    धर्म एव मन: कृष्णे स्वभावाच्चैव मे धृतम् ।
    धर्मवाणिज्यको हीनो जघन्यो धर्मवादिनाम् ॥

                             Mahābhārata, Vanaparva, 31.2.5

9. भिद्यते हृदयग्रन्थिश्छिद्यन्ते सर्वसंशया: ।
    क्षीयन्ते चास्य कर्माणि तस्मिनदृष्टे परावरे ॥

                             Muṇḍakopaniṣad, 2.2.8

10. उत्तमो ब्रह्मसद्भावो ध्यानभावस्तु मध्यम: ।
     स्तुतिर्जपोऽधमो भावो बहि: पूजाऽधमाधमा ॥

                            Mahānirvāṇa Tantra, 4.12

11. न तत्र सूर्यो भाति न चन्द्रतारकं
     नेमा विद्युतो भान्ति कुतोऽयमग्नि: ॥
     तमेव भान्तमनुभाति सर्वं
     तस्य भासा सर्वमिदं विभाति ॥

                               Kathopaniṣad, 2.2.15

12. मयि सर्वमिदं प्रोतं सूत्रे मणिगणा इव ।

                                     Gītā, 7.7

13. यद्यद्विभूतिमत् सत्त्वं श्रीमदूर्जितमेव वा ।
     तत्तदेवावगच्छ त्वं मम तेजोंऽशसम्भवम् ॥

                                  Gītā, 10.41

14. अन्तरा चापि तु तद्दृष्टे: ।

                                Vedānta Sūtra, 3.4.36